These Will Get You The Job!

15 Top Qualities Employers Look For In Job Candidates

J Cleveland Payne

Copyright © 2023 J Cleveland Payne

All rights reserved.

ISBN: 9798872599302

DEDICATION

This book is dedicated to all the people who decide to step out on faith, stepping out into the unknown of the strange job market we are living through. Don't let your current job keep you from the desired job that seems out of reach. It might not be so far out of reach as you believe.

ACKNOWLEDGMENTS

This book could not have come together without the love and support of my wife, Kristina. She may not understand the motivation behind many (or any) of my projects, but she still gives me the blessing to pursue and a shoulder to cry on when they don't play out as planned.

Table Of Contents

Why These Fifteen Traits?...1
Trait #1: Ambition..7
Trait #2: Communication..13
Trait #3: Confidence 19
Trait #4: Critical Thinking...25
Trait #5: Dependability 31
Trait #6: Determination...37
Trait #7: Eagerness to Learn 43
Trait #8: Flexibility 49
Trait #9: Honesty 55
Trait #10: Loyalty..61
Trait #11: Positivity...67
Trait #12: Problem-Solving 73
Trait #13: Self-Reliance..79
Trait #14: Teamwork 85
Trait #15: Work Ethic..91
When These Qualities Become Problems 97
About The Author...105
About The Podcasts..109

Why These Fifteen Traits?
Use This Book To Improve Yourself & Understand The Pitfalls Of Being A Good Worker

I have studied how people act in groups and workplaces since high school. Formally, since I was planning on going into the military, I was studying personalities and leadership, but always having an eye on how others get work done helps or hurts the leaders of a group, and how a leader can engage in encouraging more of the good and less of the bad.

I served in the military but not in a command role, which led to my short time on active duty. While it took me a while to formally get a job in education, I still maintained study in workers' behavior as I pursued a side hustle in the professional development of young people joining the workforce, and have helped dozens of people over the years package themselves so they can break out of careers they feel stuck in.

Now that I have recently gotten a job teaching Entrepreneurial Studies classes at the university level, I now have the 'plausible deniability' to put many of my ideas down in print with less fear of others taking the notion that my gripes or celebrations of people and their actions point to anyone in particular because everyone will take the smallest slight or cheer as a personal endorsement.

With that in mind, I have helped people focus on plenty of traits in my time. Eight months before completing this book, I whittled down the sprawling list I had used in the past to this list of fifteen. Some traits became amalgams of a few similar ones; some just had to be discarded; otherwise, I would never come to an end.

These fifteen traits are not the ultimate list of traits to master, but when interviewing hiring managers and supervisors, these traits come up routinely in conversation.

Trait #1: Ambition

The desire for personal achievement or distinction.

Trait #2: Communication

The exchange of information through a common system of symbols, signs, or behaviors.

Trait #3: Confidence

A feeling of self-assurance arising from an appreciation of one's abilities.

Trait #4: Critical Thinking

The objective analysis and evaluation of an issue to form a judgment.

Trait #5: Dependability

The quality of being trustworthy and reliable.

Trait #6: Determination

The possession of firmness of purpose and resoluteness.

Trait #7: Eagerness to Learn

The keen desire to gain knowledge or skills.

Trait #8: Flexibility

The ability to adapt to new, different, or changing requirements.

Trait #9: Honesty

The quality of being truthful and free from deceit.

Trait #10: Loyalty

The strong feeling of allegiance or support.

Trait #11: Positivity

The practice of being optimistic in attitude.

Trait #12: Problem-Solving

The process of finding solutions to difficult or complex issues.

Trait #13: Self-Reliance

Reliance on one's own powers and resources rather than those of others.

Trait #14: Teamwork

The combined action of a group, especially when effective and efficient.

Trait #15: Work Ethic

A set of values centered on the importance of doing work and reflected in a determination or desire to work hard.

Please use this book as a guide to help you understand the nature of all fifteen of these traits and learn how to improve them in yourself and present them to employers--both current and possible future ones. This will help you advance in your career to unimaginable heights.

And then, please use this book to create a simple defense for the off chance that you find yourself working not for a rational employer who wants the best for their company and will allow you the best for yourself to help get there. You are probably reading this book because your current employer has you in a less-than-desirable work situation, and you are looking to improve your skills to help you break out. After going through all fifteen traits with details on learning and growing, I will offer you a short list of red flags to look for.

Please feel free to reach out with questions and comments on any part of this book. If you have any questions on a topic, comments on my conclusions, or want to chat, reach out to me via the Business Question Answered Here email account at businessquestionsansweredhere@gmail.com or at jclevelandpayne@gmail.com. I hope to have a 'more better' website updated soon with links to the podcast and weekly essays at businessquestionsansweredhere.com.

Trait #1: Ambition

The Driving Force in Your Career

When we talk about the qualities that employers seek in job candidates, 'Ambition' often tops the list. But why is ambition so valued, and how can it shape your career trajectory? This chapter delves into the essence of ambition, illustrating why it's a crucial trait for anyone aiming to thrive in their professional life.

Understanding Ambition

At its core, ambition is more than just a desire for success. It's a deep-seated drive that propels individuals towards their goals. Ambitious people don't just aspire to be good; they strive to be great. They are not content with the status quo; they are always looking for ways to improve and excel.

Why Employers Value Ambition

- **Indication of Motivation and Dedication:** Employers see ambition as a sign of a candidate's inherent motivation and dedication. Ambitious individuals are self-starters, often going above and beyond what is required.
- **Growth Mindset:** Ambitious people typically possess a growth mindset. They see challenges as opportunities to learn and grow, rather than as insurmountable obstacles. This attitude is infectious and can inspire a culture of continuous improvement within an organization.
- **Long-term Potential:** An ambitious employee is seen as a long-term asset. Employers are aware

that ambitious individuals are likely to seek out opportunities for professional development, making them valuable players in the company's future.
- **Leadership Qualities:** Ambition is closely tied to leadership. Ambitious individuals often take initiative, show resilience in the face of adversity, and have a clear vision – all essential qualities of effective leaders.

How to Showcase Your Ambition

- **Share Your Goals:** During interviews or networking events, openly discuss your professional goals. Let potential employers see the bigger picture you have for your career. This transparency not only shows ambition but also helps employers understand how your aspirations align with their organizational goals.
- **Demonstrate a Track Record of Achievement:** Provide concrete examples of how your ambition has driven you to achieve noteworthy results in the past. This could be through leadership roles, projects you've spearheaded, or challenges you've overcome.
- **Show Enthusiasm for Learning and Growth:** Express your eagerness to learn and take on new challenges. Employers value candidates who are not just looking for a job, but are seeking a role in which they can grow and contribute significantly.
- **Be Curious and Ask Questions:** Show genuine interest in the industry, the company, and its challenges. This demonstrates that you are

thinking ahead and are keen to engage with complex issues.

Balancing Ambition

While ambition is a vital trait, balancing it is equally important. Overly ambitious individuals can sometimes come across as aggressive or single-minded, which can be off-putting to some employers. The key is to channel your ambition in a way that is productive, collaborative, and aligned with the company's values and goals.

Cultivating Ambition

If you feel your ambition needs a boost, consider the following steps:

- **Set Clear Goals:** Define what success looks like to you. Set both short-term and long-term goals, and create a roadmap to achieve them.
- **Seek Inspiration:** Surround yourself with ambitious people, whether it's through professional networks, mentors, or industry leaders. Their drive can be contagious.
- **Embrace Challenges:** Step out of your comfort zone and take on tasks that stretch your abilities. This not only shows ambition but also helps in personal and professional growth.
- **Stay Informed:** Keep up-to-date with industry trends and advancements. A well-informed candidate is often seen as an ambitious one.

Ambition is the fuel that drives career advancement. It's about having a vision for your future and the determination to turn that vision into reality. By demonstrating your ambition, you not only increase your appeal to potential employers but also set the stage for a fulfilling and dynamic career. Remember, ambition is not just about reaching the top; it's about the journey and the growth that happens along the way. Share your dreams, stay motivated, and let your ambition shine – it's a key ingredient to unlocking your full professional potential.

Trait #2: Communication

The Heart of Professional Success

In the realm of sought-after qualities in job candidates, effective communication stands out as a cornerstone. This chapter explores why stellar communication skills are a non-negotiable in the professional world and how you can demonstrate and enhance these skills to align with employers' expectations.

The Essence of Effective Communication

Communication is not just about conveying information; it's about ensuring that the message is understood and acted upon effectively. It's a two-way street that involves expressing thoughts clearly and listening attentively. In the workplace, this skill is vital for teamwork, problem-solving, and building relationships.

Why Employers Value Communication

- **Fosters Collaboration:** Clear communication is the key to effective teamwork. Employers look for individuals who can articulate their ideas and also understand others' perspectives to foster a collaborative work environment.
- **Facilitates Problem-Solving:** The ability to discuss problems and brainstorm solutions in a clear and structured way is crucial in any professional setting.
- **Ensures Efficiency:** Good communication minimizes misunderstandings and errors, leading to a more efficient workflow.

- **Builds Professional Relationships:** Strong communication skills are essential for building rapport with colleagues, clients, and stakeholders.
- **Reflects Professionalism:** Your communication style can significantly impact how you are perceived professionally. Clear, concise, and respectful communication is often seen as a sign of competence and confidence.

Demonstrating Communication Skills

- **Verbal Communication: Speak** clearly and confidently. Tailor your language to your audience and avoid jargon when it's not appropriate. Practice public speaking or engage in activities that require verbal communication to refine this skill.
- **Non-Verbal Communication:** Your body language, eye contact, and facial expressions speak volumes. Be mindful of these, especially in interviews or meetings, as they can reinforce or undermine your verbal message.
- **Written Communication:** In emails, reports, and even texts, be clear, concise, and grammatically correct. Proofread your work to avoid errors that can detract from your professionalism.
- **Active Listening:** Show that you are engaged in conversations by maintaining eye contact, nodding, and providing feedback. This demonstrates respect and interest in what others are saying.

- **Providing Feedback:** Offer constructive feedback when required. Be honest yet respectful, focusing on the issue rather than the person.

Enhancing Your Communication Skills

- **Seek Feedback:** Ask for feedback on your communication style from peers or mentors. This can provide insights into areas for improvement.
- **Engage in Diverse Conversations:** Interact with a wide range of people. This exposure can enhance your ability to communicate effectively with different personalities and in various contexts.
- **Attend Workshops or Courses:** Consider enrolling in workshops or courses that focus on improving communication skills.
- **Practice Empathy:** Try to understand things from others' perspectives. This can significantly improve how you interact and respond in conversations.

The Role of Technology in Communication

In today's digital age, understanding how to communicate effectively through various platforms, such as emails, social media, and virtual meetings, is increasingly important. Employers value candidates who can adapt their communication style to these different mediums.

Avoiding Common Communication Pitfalls

- **Over-communicating:** Bombarding colleagues with messages or information can be overwhelming. Be concise.
- **Under-communicating:** Conversely, providing too little information can lead to misunderstandings. Ensure that your message is complete.
- **Neglecting the Tone:** In written communication, it's easy to misinterpret the tone. Be mindful of how your words might come across.
- **Ignoring Cultural Differences:** In today's globalized world, being sensitive to cultural nuances in communication is crucial.

Effective communication is a multifaceted skill that encompasses speaking, listening, writing, and non-verbal cues. It's about clarity, empathy, and understanding the context. In your job search and professional life, showcase your communication prowess through your resume, cover letter, and interviews. Remember, good communication is not just about talking; it's equally about listening and understanding. By honing these skills, you're not just enhancing your employability; you're setting yourself up for long-term professional success and meaningful workplace relationships. Communication is indeed the heartbeat of the professional world, and mastering it can open doors to endless opportunities.

Trait #3: Confidence

Your Gateway to Professional Excellence

When sifting through potential candidates, employers aren't just looking for skills and experience; they're also seeking individuals who exude confidence. This chapter dives into why confidence is a prized trait in the professional arena and how it can be the key to unlocking your career potential.

The Role of Confidence in the Workplace

Confidence is not just about believing in yourself; it's about projecting that belief in a way that convinces others. It's a magnetic quality that can influence how you are perceived by your colleagues and superiors. Confident individuals are often seen as more competent, trustworthy, and capable of handling responsibilities effectively.

Why Employers Value Confidence

- **Positive Impact on Team Dynamics:** Confident employees tend to be more positive and proactive, which can significantly boost team morale and productivity.
- **Enhanced Decision-Making:** Confidence is closely linked to decisiveness. Employers value employees who can make informed decisions quickly and stand by them.
- **Leadership Potential:** Confidence is a cornerstone of leadership. Those who are confident in their abilities are often naturally

inclined to take on leadership roles and inspire others.
- **Ability to Handle Challenges:** Confident individuals are generally better equipped to handle workplace challenges and setbacks without losing their morale.
- **Effective Communication:** Confidence shines through in how individuals communicate. It helps in articulating thoughts more clearly and convincingly.

Developing and Demonstrating Confidence

- **Know Your Strengths (and Weaknesses):** Understand what you're good at and what areas need improvement. Being aware of your capabilities and limitations is a critical aspect of confidence.
- **Set Clear Goals:** Having clear professional goals and articulating them effectively to potential employers shows that you're not just after any job, but are striving for something that aligns with your aspirations.
- **Body Language:** Your posture, eye contact, and hand gestures can reflect confidence. Practice good body language to reinforce your verbal communication.
- **Prepare and Practice:** Be it for an interview, a presentation, or a meeting, preparation boosts confidence. The more prepared you are, the more confident you'll feel.
- **Seek Feedback:** Constructive feedback can help you understand how others perceive you and where you can improve.

- **Embrace Challenges:** Stepping out of your comfort zone and tackling new challenges can significantly build your confidence.

The Balance of Confidence

While confidence is vital, it's important to strike a balance. Overconfidence can be perceived as arrogance, which can be off-putting to employers and colleagues. True confidence is paired with humility and the willingness to learn and grow.

Confidence in Communication

Effective communication is a clear indicator of confidence. Being able to express your thoughts and ideas clearly and respectfully is a sign of a confident individual. Practice active listening and clear, concise speaking to enhance this aspect.

Confidence and Resilience

Resilience goes hand in hand with confidence. Being able to bounce back from setbacks and maintain your confidence is crucial. Employers value individuals who can remain confident and positive even in challenging situations.

Building Confidence Over Time

Confidence is not an innate trait; it can be developed and strengthened over time. Engage in activities that challenge you, seek roles that require you to step up, and continuously work on your personal and professional development.

Overcoming Confidence Roadblocks

Everyone faces moments of self-doubt. Recognize these moments and work through them. Seek support from mentors or peers, and remember that every professional, at some point, has faced and overcome similar challenges.

Showcasing Confidence in Job Searches

- Resume and Cover Letter: Use these tools to confidently articulate your achievements and skills. Highlight experiences that showcase your confidence in handling various tasks and roles.
- Interviews: Use interviews as an opportunity to demonstrate your confidence. Answer questions clearly and confidently, and don't shy away from discussing your achievements.
- Networking: Confidently engage in networking opportunities. Show genuine interest in others and share your experiences and aspirations openly.

Confidence is a dynamic and influential quality that can set you apart in the professional world. It's about knowing your worth, understanding your abilities, and having the assurance to put them into action. Remember, confidence is not about having all the answers; it's about being open to finding them. Cultivate confidence through continuous learning, self-awareness, and embracing challenges. As you step into the professional world, let your confidence be the beacon that guides you to opportunities and helps you turn them into successes.

Trait #4: Critical Thinking

The Key to Problem-Solving Excellence

In the dynamic and often complex world of work, critical thinking stands out as a highly sought-after skill. This chapter will explore why critical thinking is essential in the workplace and how it can significantly impact your professional journey.

Understanding Critical Thinking

Critical thinking is not just a methodical approach to problem-solving; it's a disciplined way of thinking that involves analyzing, evaluating, and synthesizing information in a logical and unbiased manner. It's about being curious, asking the right questions, and being open to new perspectives and solutions.

Why Employers Value Critical Thinking

- **Enhances Problem-Solving Skills:** Critical thinkers can dissect complex problems and devise effective solutions. Employers value this ability to navigate challenges efficiently and innovatively.
- **Facilitates Decision-Making:** In decision-making, critical thinkers can weigh all aspects, consider various outcomes, and choose the most effective course of action.
- **Promotes Innovation:** By questioning norms and thinking outside the box, critical thinkers can drive innovation and push the boundaries of what's possible in their field.

- **Encourages Independence:** Good critical thinkers can work independently, making well-thought-out decisions without constant supervision.
- **Improves Team Collaboration:** Critical thinking is not a solitary skill. When applied in team settings, it can enhance group problem-solving and decision-making.

Developing Critical Thinking Skills

- **Ask Questions:** Be inquisitive. Asking questions helps in understanding the problem more deeply and prompts you to consider different perspectives.
- **Gather Information:** Collect relevant data and information before jumping to conclusions. This step is crucial for informed decision-making.
- **Analyze and Interpret Data:** Look for patterns, trends, and connections. Analyzing information helps in understanding the underlying issues.
- **Consider Different Viewpoints:** Be open to different perspectives. This can provide a more rounded view of the problem and possible solutions.
- **Evaluate Evidence:** Assess the reliability and credibility of the information you gather. Not all information is created equal.
- **Reflect on Your Biases:** Be aware of your own biases and how they might affect your thinking process. Strive for objectivity.

Critical Thinking in Action

- **Problem-Solving:** When faced with a problem, use a structured approach. Break the problem down into smaller parts and tackle each part methodically.
- **Decision-Making:** In decision-making, consider the pros and cons of each option. Think about the short-term and long-term implications of your decision.
- **Innovation and Creativity:** Use critical thinking to challenge the status quo and come up with innovative ideas or solutions.
- **Collaboration:** In team settings, encourage open discussion and debate. Listen to others' viewpoints and integrate them into your thinking process.

Enhancing Critical Thinking in the Workplace

- **Continuous Learning:** Keep updating your knowledge and skills. A well-informed mind is better equipped for critical thinking.
- **Seek Feedback:** Regular feedback can help you understand different perspectives and improve your thinking process.
- **Practice Problem-Solving:** Engage in activities or take on projects that challenge your problem-solving skills.
- **Reflect on Your Experiences:** Take time to reflect on your decisions and their outcomes. This can provide valuable insights for future situations.

Showcasing Critical Thinking Skills in Your Job Search

- **Resume and Cover Letter:** Highlight instances where you've successfully applied critical thinking to solve problems or make decisions.
- **Interviews:** Be prepared to discuss specific examples of how you've used critical thinking in your professional life.
- **Portfolios or Case Studies:** If applicable, include portfolios or case studies that showcase your ability to think critically and solve complex problems.

Overcoming Obstacles to Critical Thinking

- **Avoid Jumping to Conclusions:** Take the time to analyze all aspects of a problem before forming an opinion.
- **Don't Overlook Details:** Sometimes, small details can have a big impact on the outcome. Pay attention to them.
- **Resist Groupthink:** In team settings, don't be afraid to voice a different opinion. Diversity of thought is crucial to effective critical thinking.

Critical thinking is more than a skill; it's a mindset that can significantly enhance your professional capabilities. It's about being curious, methodical, and open-minded. In a world where problems are often complex and solutions are not black and white, the ability to think critically is invaluable. By honing this skill, you not only become a more attractive candidate to potential employers but also equip yourself with a tool that will be beneficial throughout your career. Remember, at its heart, critical thinking is about making reasoned judgments that are logical and well-thought-out. It's a skill that will serve you well in any professional journey you embark upon.

Trait #5: Dependability

The Foundation of Professional Trust

In the quest to find the ideal job candidate, employers often prioritize dependability. This chapter explores the essence of dependability in the workplace and how it can be a decisive factor in your professional success.

What is Dependability?

Dependability is the quality of being trustworthy and reliable. In a professional context, it means being someone your team and employer can count on. A dependable person consistently meets deadlines, maintains punctuality, and upholds a strong work ethic. It's about commitment, consistency, and the ability to follow through on promises.

Why Employers Value Dependability

- **Ensures Consistency:** Dependable employees bring a level of consistency to their work that is invaluable. They are the ones who stabilize teams and projects.
- **Builds Trust:** When you're dependable, your colleagues and superiors trust you with responsibilities, knowing that you will deliver.
- **Promotes Team Efficiency:** A dependable team member enhances the overall efficiency of the group, ensuring smooth workflow and project completion.
- **Reflects Professionalism:** Being dependable is a hallmark of professionalism. It shows that you

take your job seriously and are committed to your role.
- **Facilitates Better Planning and Execution:** Teams can plan and execute tasks more effectively when they include dependable members.

Demonstrating Dependability

- **Meet Deadlines:** Make it a point to complete tasks on or before their due dates. This shows that you're organized and value the time of others.
- **Be Punctual:** Whether it's arriving on time for work or meetings, punctuality is a key aspect of dependability.
- **Follow Through on Commitments:** If you've committed to a task, ensure you see it through. This builds your reputation as someone who can be relied upon.
- **Communicate Proactively:** Keep your team and supervisors informed about your progress. If you foresee delays, communicate them early.
- **Maintain Consistent Quality of Work:** Ensure that the quality of your work doesn't falter, regardless of the task's size or significance.

Building a Dependable Reputation

- **Start Small:** Build your reputation by reliably handling small tasks before taking on larger responsibilities.
- **Organize and Prioritize:** Use tools and methods to keep your tasks organized. Prioritize your work to meet deadlines effectively.

- **Be Proactive:** Don't wait for reminders. Take initiative in completing your tasks and offering help when you see an opportunity.
- **Seek Feedback:** Regular feedback can help you understand how others perceive your dependability and where you can improve.
- **Learn to Say No:** Overcommitting can harm your dependability. Learn to say no when you know you can't meet the expectations.

Showcasing Dependability During the Job Search

- **In Your Resume:** Highlight instances where your dependability made a difference in your previous roles. Quantify these instances if possible.
- **During Interviews:** Share specific examples of situations where your dependability positively impacted your team or project.
- **Through References:** Choose references who can vouch for your dependability. Their testimonials can be powerful endorsements of your reliability.

Dependability in Remote Work

In today's increasingly remote work environment, dependability takes on new dimensions. It's about being reachable, meeting deadlines despite physical absence, and maintaining consistent communication.

Balancing Dependability with Flexibility

While being dependable is crucial, it's also important to balance it with flexibility. Be ready to adapt to changing circumstances and unexpected challenges while maintaining your reliability.

Overcoming Challenges to Dependability

- **Time Management Issues:** If time management is a barrier to your dependability, consider using techniques like the Eisenhower Box or Pomodoro Technique.
- **Handling Work Overload:** Learn to delegate and communicate your workload to your supervisor to maintain the quality and timeliness of your work.
- **Personal Challenges:** If personal issues are affecting your dependability, communicate with your employer to find a viable solution.

Dependability is a cornerstone of a strong professional character. It's not just about doing your job; it's about doing it with a sense of responsibility and reliability. This quality doesn't just benefit your employer; it enriches your professional life, opening doors to more opportunities and fostering a sense of accomplishment and pride in your work. As you step into or progress in your career, let dependability be a defining trait of your professional identity. Remember, in the eyes of an employer, a dependable employee is an invaluable asset.

Trait #6: Determination
The Drive to Achieve Success

In the employment landscape, determination stands out as a vital attribute employers actively seek in candidates. This chapter delves into the essence of determination and how it can significantly shape your professional journey.

Understanding Determination

Determination is the steadfast pursuit of goals despite obstacles and setbacks. The inner strength that drives you to push through challenges and keep moving towards your objectives. In the workplace, determination often separates those who achieve their goals from those who fall short.

Why Employers Value Determination

- **Overcomes Challenges:** Determined individuals are not easily discouraged by setbacks. They are the ones who find ways to overcome obstacles, making them invaluable in challenging work environments.
- **Fuels Persistence:** Determination is synonymous with persistence. Employers value candidates who can stay the course until a project is successfully completed.
- **Drives Professional Growth:** A determined person is often a self-motivated learner and achiever, continually seeking to improve and advance in their career.

- **Encourages Innovation:** Determination pushes individuals to look for innovative solutions when faced with complex problems.
- **Builds Resilience:** Determined employees tend to be more resilient, capable of handling stress and rebounding from failures or disappointments.

Demonstrating Determination

- **Share Your Success Stories:** During interviews, share specific examples of how your determination helped you overcome challenges and achieve goals.
- **Set and Achieve Goals:** Regularly set personal and professional goals and make the necessary effort to achieve them. This habit demonstrates your determination.
- **Be Persistent:** Show persistence in your job search and career. Follow up on job applications and continue developing your skills even when faced with rejection.
- **Display a Positive Attitude:** Approach challenges with a can-do attitude. A positive approach often reflects a determined mindset.
- **Learn from Failures:** When discussing past failures, focus on what you learned and how you used the experience to grow and improve.

Cultivating Determination

- **Set Clear Goals:** Having clear, achievable goals gives you a target to focus your determination on.

- **Develop a Plan:** Create a roadmap for achieving your goals. A well-thought-out plan can help maintain your determination.
- **Stay Motivated:** Find what motivates you and keep that in your mind, especially during challenging times.
- **Build Resilience:** Work on developing resilience so that setbacks don't derail your determination.
- **Seek Inspiration:** Surround yourself with stories and people who inspire determination. Sometimes, seeing examples of obstinacy in others can ignite it in ourselves.

Determination in the Workplace

- **Meet Challenges Head-On:** Embrace workplace challenges as opportunities to showcase your determination.
- **Take Initiative:** Taking the initiative on projects or to solve problems at work can be a strong demonstration of determination.
- **Show Commitment to Quality:** Consistently producing high-quality work despite difficult circumstances displays determination.
- **Be a Team Motivator:** Use your determination to motivate and inspire your team, especially when facing challenging projects or tight deadlines.

Balancing Determination with Flexibility

While determination is crucial, balancing it with flexibility is equally important. Being too rigid in your determination can sometimes lead to missed opportunities or failure to adapt to changing circumstances.

Overcoming Obstacles to Determination

- Handling Burnout: Recognize the signs of burnout and take steps to address them head-on. Determination is not about working yourself to exhaustion.
- Dealing with Doubt: When doubt creeps in, remind yourself of past successes and the goals you're working towards.
- Facing Fear of Failure: Understand that failure is a part of the journey. Use fear as a motivator rather than an obstacle.

Showcasing Determination in Your Career Path

- In Your Resume: Highlight experiences in your resume where your determination led to positive outcomes or the successful completion of projects.
- In Interviews: Be prepared to go into detail with times when someone tested your determination and how you responded.
- Through Professional Development: Continually improving your skills and knowledge base shows determination in your professional growth.

Determination is more than just a trait. It is a driving force in your career. It is about having the grit and resilience to face challenges head-on and keep going until you achieve your objectives. Let your determination be the guiding force, whether you're just starting your career or looking to make a significant change.

Remember, it often comes down to determination that makes the difference between a dream and a reality. So, as you navigate your professional path, embrace and cultivate this invaluable quality. It will make you a more attractive candidate to potential employers and empower you to reach the heights of your professional aspirations.

Trait #7: Eagerness to Learn

The Pathway to Continuous Growth

In a rapidly evolving work environment, the eagerness to learn emerges as a key quality that employers seek in candidates. This chapter will explore why a love for learning is so valued in the workplace and how it can be a major driver in your career development.

Why Employers Value Eagerness to Learn

- **Adaptability:** Employees who are eager to learn adapt more easily to changes and new technologies, making them invaluable in today's fast-paced business world.
- **Continuous Improvement:** A willingness to learn signifies a commitment to continuous self-improvement, leading to personal and organizational growth.
- **Innovation:** Learners often bring fresh ideas and perspectives, fueling innovation and creative problem-solving in the workplace.
- **Future Potential:** Employers see individuals who are committed to learning as having greater potential for future leadership roles.
- **Positive Work Attitude:** Eagerness to learn is often associated with a positive attitude and a proactive work approach.

Communicating Your Eagerness to Learn

- **Share Your Learning Experiences:** During interviews, discuss how you've pursued learning

opportunities, such as professional courses, workshops, or self-study.
- **Discuss Reading Habits:** Mention if you're an avid reader, especially of books that pertain to your field or professional development.
- **Highlight Continuous Education:** If you are pursuing or have completed additional certifications or degrees, bring these up as evidence of your commitment to learning.
- **Show Curiosity:** Ask insightful questions during interviews, showing your interest in learning more about the company, its challenges, and the industry.
- **Describe Learning Outcomes:** Explain how your learning experiences have directly impacted your professional abilities and contributed to your previous roles.

Cultivating an Eagerness to Learn

- **Set Learning Goals:** Identify areas for growth and set specific learning objectives.
- **Seek Opportunities for Professional Development:** Take advantage of workshops, webinars, and courses offered by your employer or professional associations.
- **Embrace Challenges:** View new challenges as opportunities to learn rather than obstacles.
- **Learn from Others:** Seek mentorship and guidance from more experienced colleagues.
- **Stay Updated:** Keep abreast of the latest trends and developments in your field.

Learning in the Workplace

- **Participate in Training Programs:** Show enthusiasm for company-sponsored training and development programs.
- **Volunteer for New Projects:** Demonstrate your willingness to learn by volunteering for projects that require new skills or knowledge.
- **Share Knowledge:** Be willing to share your learning with colleagues, which can foster a culture of learning within the team.
- **Apply New Skills:** Actively apply new skills and knowledge to your work, demonstrating the practical benefits of your learning.

Demonstrating Eagerness to Learn on Your Resume

- **List Relevant Courses and Certifications:** Include any additional courses or certifications you've obtained that are relevant to the job.
- **Describe Learning-Related Achievements:** Highlight any accomplishments that directly resulted from your learning efforts.
- **Mention Memberships in Professional Associations:** Being part of industry groups can show a commitment to staying connected and informed.

Overcoming Barriers to Learning

- **Time Management:** Balance your work and learning commitments. Prioritize and allocate specific times for learning.
- **Fear of Failure:** Understand that failure is part of the learning process. Embrace it as a learning opportunity.

- **Staying Motivated:** Keep reminding yourself of the long-term benefits of your learning efforts.

Integrating Learning into Your Career Path

- **Seek Roles That Offer Learning Opportunities:** During job searches, look for positions and companies that emphasize employee development and learning.
- **Discuss Learning During Interviews:** Talk about how you plan to continue learning in the role you're applying for.
- **Create a Personal Development Plan:** Have a clear plan for your professional development, including learning objectives and strategies.

Your eagerness to learn is not just an asset to potential employers; it's a cornerstone of your professional development. In a world where change is constant, the ability to continuously acquire new knowledge and skills is invaluable. By demonstrating your love for learning, you show employers that you are someone who is not just prepared for the challenges of today but is also gearing up for the opportunities of tomorrow. Remember, learning is a journey, not a destination. Embrace this journey with enthusiasm and commitment, and watch as it opens doors to unimagined possibilities in your career.

Trait #8: Flexibility

Adapting to the Ever-Changing Workplace

In today's fast-paced and ever-evolving work environment, flexibility has become a critical quality for job candidates. This chapter delves into the importance of adaptability in the workplace and how you can demonstrate and enhance this vital skill.

Understanding Flexibility

Flexibility in the professional context means the ability to adapt to changing circumstances and expectations. It's about being open to new ideas, approaches, and working conditions. Whether it's adjusting your work hours, switching to a remote setting, or taking on different responsibilities, flexibility reflects your capacity to navigate and embrace change.

Why Employers Value Flexibility

- **Responds to Changing Business Needs:** Flexible employees can quickly adjust to new strategies, helping the company stay competitive and responsive.
- **Enhances Team Dynamics:** Flexible team members can work under various conditions and with different team compositions, contributing to a more dynamic and versatile team.
- **Improves Problem-Solving:** Those who are flexible often approach challenges with a more open and creative mindset, leading to innovative solutions.

- **Facilitates Work-Life Balance:** Flexibility can also mean understanding and adapting to colleagues' needs, which fosters a more supportive and balanced work environment.
- **Indicates Emotional Intelligence:** Being flexible often requires understanding and empathy, which are key components of emotional intelligence.

Demonstrating Flexibility

- **Be Open to Change:** Show willingness to adapt to new roles, tools, or processes. Embrace change rather than resist it.
- **Share Past Experiences:** Discuss times when you successfully adapted to significant changes at work, highlighting your ability to remain productive and positive.
- **Exhibit Versatility:** Demonstrate a range of skills and the ability to handle different types of tasks and responsibilities.
- **Show Initiative in Problem-Solving:** Be proactive in addressing issues and suggesting improvements. This can demonstrate your ability to think flexibly and adaptively.
- **Adapt Communication Style:** Show that you can communicate effectively with different people and in various situations.

Cultivating Flexibility

- **Develop a Growth Mindset:** Embrace learning and view challenges as opportunities to grow.

- **Practice Resilience:** Build your capacity to recover from setbacks. Resilience is a key part of being flexible.
- **Stay Informed and Prepared:** Keep abreast of industry trends and potential changes in your field. Being informed helps you adapt more quickly.
- **Work on Emotional Intelligence:** Improving your emotional intelligence can enhance your ability to empathize and adapt to social dynamics.
- **Learn New Skills:** Continuously expand your skill set. This makes it easier to adapt to new roles or responsibilities.

Flexibility in Different Work Settings

- **In the Office:** Be willing to take on different tasks or work extra hours when needed.
- **While Working Remotely:** Adapt to virtual communication and collaboration tools. Show that you can remain productive and connected, even from afar.
- **In Hybrid Environments:** Demonstrate your ability to seamlessly transition between remote and in-office work.

Showing Flexibility During the Job Search

- **In Your Resume:** Highlight experiences that demonstrate your adaptability, such as working in different roles or environments.
- **During Interviews:** Be prepared to discuss how you've adapted to changes in the past and how you handle ambiguity and uncertainty.

- **Through References:** Choose references who can speak to your ability to adapt and thrive in changing environments.

Balancing Flexibility with Boundaries

While being flexible is important, it's equally crucial to set healthy boundaries. Know your limits and communicate them clearly to prevent burnout and maintain work-life balance.

Overcoming Challenges to Flexibility

- **Dealing with Uncertainty:** Learn to be comfortable with not having all the answers and develop strategies to cope with uncertainty.
- **Managing Stress:** Develop stress management techniques to help you stay calm and composed during times of change.
- **Avoiding Overcommitment:** Learn to say no when necessary. Overcommitting can hinder your ability to remain flexible.

Flexibility is not just a skill; it's a mindset that empowers you to thrive in a variety of situations and roles. In the modern workplace, the ability to adapt is as important as any technical skill or experience. By cultivating and demonstrating flexibility, you not only make yourself a more attractive candidate to potential employers but also equip yourself to navigate the complexities and uncertainties of today's job market. Remember, the most successful professionals are those who can bend without breaking, adapting to new challenges with resilience and a positive attitude.

Trait #9: Honesty

The Bedrock of Professional Integrity

In the mosaic of qualities that form an ideal job candidate, honesty shines as a fundamental trait. This chapter delves into the importance of honesty in the workplace and how it can profoundly impact your career.

Understanding Honesty

Honesty in a professional context means being truthful about your qualifications, experiences, and actions. It's not just about not lying; it's about being authentic and genuine. Honesty reflects your moral character and can build or erode trust in your professional relationships.

Why Employers Value Honesty

- **Builds Trust:** Honesty is the foundation of trust in any relationship, including the professional ones. Employers need to trust that their staff will be truthful and transparent.
- **Ensures Reliability:** Honest employees are viewed as reliable and responsible, qualities that are essential in a productive workplace.
- **Promotes a Healthy Work Environment:** An environment where honesty is valued is often more open, fair, and collaborative.
- **Fosters Ethical Standards:** Honesty is a key component of ethical behavior in the workplace, influencing decisions and actions.
- **Supports Accurate Assessment and Growth:** When employees are honest about their skills and performance, it allows for accurate

assessments and targeted professional development.

Demonstrating Honesty

- **Be Truthful in Your Resume and Interviews:** Avoid exaggerating your qualifications or experience. Be clear about what you know and what you don't.
- **Admit Mistakes:** When you make a mistake, own up to it. This demonstrates maturity and a commitment to learning and improvement.
- **Provide Honest Feedback:** When asked for your opinion, be honest yet respectful. Constructive feedback can lead to positive changes.
- **Respect Confidentiality:** Being trustworthy with sensitive information is a crucial aspect of honesty in the workplace.
- **Communicate Openly:** Be open and transparent in your communications. Clear, honest communication can prevent misunderstandings and conflicts.

The Consequences of Dishonesty

Dishonesty, even in small matters, can have significant consequences. It can lead to a loss of trust, damage to your reputation, and even legal issues. Remember, once trust is broken, it's incredibly difficult to rebuild.

Honesty Beyond the Interview

- **In the Workplace:** Continue to demonstrate honesty in all your professional dealings, whether it's in reporting your work, dealing with colleagues, or interacting with clients.

- **During Performance Reviews:** Be honest about your achievements and areas where you need improvement. This can lead to more meaningful and productive discussions about your career growth.
- **When Facing Ethical Dilemmas:** If you find yourself in a situation where honesty is challenged, stand firm in your values. The respect you'll earn is far more valuable than any short-term gain from dishonesty.

Balancing Honesty with Tact

Being honest doesn't mean being blunt or harsh. It's important to balance honesty with tact and empathy. Delivering the truth in a considerate and respectful way is a skill that enhances your professional communication.

Cultivating Honesty

- **Reflect on Your Values:** Regularly reflect on your values and how they align with your actions. This can reinforce your commitment to honesty.
- **Seek Feedback:** Ask for feedback on your honesty and integrity. This can provide insights into how you're perceived and where you can improve.
- **Practice Self-Awareness:** Be aware of situations where you might be tempted to be less than honest and prepare yourself to respond with integrity.
- **Learn from Role Models:** Observe and learn from individuals who exemplify honesty in their professional lives.

Honesty and Career Advancement

- **In Job Applications:** Be honest about your qualifications and experiences. Skills can be learned, but trust, once broken, is hard to regain.
- **In Networking:** Build your professional network with honesty. Authentic relationships are more valuable and enduring.
- **In Leadership Roles:** If you aspire to be a leader, remember that honesty is key to inspiring trust and respect in your team.

Overcoming Challenges to Honesty

- **Pressure to Conform:** If you face pressure to compromise your honesty, stand firm. Your integrity is more important than short-term gains.
- **Fear of Consequences:** Being honest, especially about mistakes, can be daunting. However, facing the consequences honestly can lead to personal and professional growth.

Honesty in the workplace goes beyond just telling the truth. It's about being a person of integrity, someone who can be relied upon to be authentic and ethical. As you navigate your career, let honesty be your guiding principle. It's a quality that will earn you respect, trust, and long-term success in your professional endeavors. In a world where dishonesty can seem prevalent, being honest can set you apart as a truly valuable asset to any organization. Remember, honesty isn't just the best policy; it's the foundation of a fulfilling and respected career.

Trait #10: Loyalty

A Commitment to Shared Success

Loyalty is a highly prized quality in a professional landscape often characterized by frequent transitions. This chapter explores the depth and significance of loyalty in the workplace and how embodying this trait can impact your career.

Understanding Loyalty

In a professional context, loyalty is more than just staying with a company for a long time. It demonstrates commitment and dedication to an organization's goals and values. A loyal employee believes in the company's mission and actively contributes towards achieving it.

Why Employers Value Loyalty

- **Promotes Stability:** Loyal employees contribute to a stable work environment. This is essential for long-term planning and growth.
- **Enhances Team Morale:** Loyalty can foster a sense of camaraderie and belonging among team members, boosting overall morale.
- **Increases Productivity:** Employees who are loyal to their company are often more motivated and engaged, leading to higher productivity.
- **Reduces Turnover Costs:** High employee turnover can be costly. Loyal employees will likely stay longer, reducing the costs and disruptions associated with hiring and training new staff.

- **Cultivates Company Culture:** Loyal employees often embody and reinforce the company's culture, playing a pivotal role in its perpetuation and evolution.

Demonstrating Loyalty

- **Show Commitment to Company Goals:** Align your work and efforts with the company's objectives. Demonstrating that you are working towards the same goals as the company is a powerful expression of loyalty.
- **Be a Positive Advocate:** Speak positively about your company in public forums. This can be as simple as sharing company successes on social media or defending your company's reputation.
- **Be Reliable and Consistent:** Consistency in your performance and reliability in your responsibilities are strong loyalty indicators.
- **Offer Constructive Feedback:** Loyalty does not mean blind allegiance. Offering constructive feedback for the company's betterment shows deep care and commitment.
- **Build Long-Term Relationships:** Foster long-term professional relationships within the company. This network can be a testament to your loyalty.

.The Benefits of Loyalty

- **Career Advancement:** Loyal employees are often first in line for promotions and additional responsibilities.
- **Professional Development:** Companies are more likely to invest in training and development for employees who have shown loyalty.

- **Greater Influence:** As a loyal employee, your opinions and suggestions might carry more weight within the organization.
- **Trust and Respect:** Loyal employees often earn a higher levels trust and respect from their colleagues and superiors.

Balancing Loyalty with Personal Growth

While loyalty is valuable, balancing it with personal growth and career aspirations is essential. Blind loyalty should not come at the cost of your professional development or well-being.

Loyalty in Today's Work Environment

- **In Start-Ups and Small Businesses:** In smaller companies, loyalty can directly impact the business's success and growth.
- **In Large Corporations:** Even in large corporations, loyalty can contribute to a sense of community and belonging, impacting the company culture positively.
- **In Remote Work:** Show loyalty in remote settings by being engaged, responsive, and proactive in your work.

Cultivating Loyalty

- **Understand the Company's Vision:** Understanding your company's vision and goals can foster a sense of alignment and loyalty.
- **Build Meaningful Connections:** Develop strong relationships with colleagues and superiors.

These connections can reinforce your commitment to the company.
- **Seek Alignment:** Look for aspects of the company's mission and values that align with your own values.
- **Voice Your Commitment:** Don't hesitate to express your commitment to the company's future in discussions with managers and team leaders.

Overcoming Challenges to Loyalty

- **Dealing with Disillusionment:** If you feel disillusioned, identify the root cause. It might be a temporary issue that can be resolved through communication.
- **Navigating Corporate Changes:** Companies evolve, and changes might challenge your sense of loyalty. Assess how these changes align with your personal values and career goals.
- **Managing Personal and Professional Balance:** Always strive for a balance. Loyalty to a company should not come at the expense of your personal life or well-being.

Loyalty and Job Searching

- **During Interviews:** Communicate your desire to grow with the company. Discuss how your long-term career goals align with the company's vision.
- **In Your Resume:** Highlight long-term roles and projects, and emphasize your contributions to your previous employers' successes.

- **Through References:** Choose references who speak to your loyalty and commitment in previous roles.

Loyalty is a multidimensional trait encompassing commitment, reliability, and a belief in your company's mission. It goes beyond the duration of your tenure; it's reflected in how you engage with your work and advocate for your organization. In an era where job-hopping is common, loyalty can set you apart as a candidate and employee who is not just looking for a job but a mission to commit to. As you navigate your career path, let loyalty be a guiding principle that balances your aspirations with a commitment to shared success.

Trait #11: Positivity

Cultivating a Constructive Work Environment

In the tapestry of attributes that create an ideal job candidate, positivity stands out as a vibrant thread. This chapter delves into the significance of a positive attitude in the workplace and how it can be a transformative force for both the individual and the organization.

Understanding Positivity

Positivity in the workplace goes beyond mere cheerfulness; it's about cultivating a constructive and optimistic outlook. It involves seeing challenges as opportunities, focusing on solutions rather than problems, and maintaining a hopeful perspective even under challenging situations.

Why Employers Value Positivity

- **Enhances Team Morale:** A positive attitude is infectious and can significantly uplift the morale of a team.
- **Fosters Resilience:** Positive individuals tend to be more resilient, bouncing back from setbacks more quickly and effectively.
- **Improves Collaboration:** People are naturally drawn to positive individuals, making collaboration more enjoyable and productive.
- **Drives Engagement:** A positive work environment encourages greater employee engagement and dedication.
- **Boosts Creativity:** Positivity has been linked to higher levels of creativity, as it encourages open-

mindedness and a willingness to explore new ideas.

Demonstrating Positivity

- **Maintain a Constructive Outlook:** Focus on solutions and opportunities for growth, rather than dwelling on problems.
- **Be Supportive and Encouraging:** Offer support and encouragement to colleagues, recognizing their efforts and achievements.
- **Handle Challenges Gracefully:** When faced with setbacks, approach them with calm and optimism, showing your ability to manage difficulties constructively.
- **Spread Goodwill:** Engage in acts of kindness and positivity, whether it's through a supportive word or a helpful gesture.
- **Express Gratitude:** Show appreciation for your colleagues and the opportunities you receive at work.

Cultivating a Positive Attitude

- **Practice Mindfulness:** Mindfulness techniques can help maintain a positive outlook by reducing stress and promoting emotional balance.
- **Develop Emotional Intelligence:** Understanding and managing your emotions can contribute to a more positive attitude.
- **Seek Positive Influences:** Surround yourself with positive people and content, as they can influence your own mindset.

- **Reflect on Positives:** Regularly reflect on the positive aspects of your work and life, however small they may be.
- **Embrace Continuous Learning:** View challenges as opportunities to learn and grow, which can foster a positive outlook.

The Power of Positivity in Teams

- **Enhance Team Dynamics:** Your positive attitude can inspire and uplift your team, leading to better teamwork and higher morale.
- **Lead by Example:** Model positivity for others. Your approach can set the tone for the entire team.
- **Encourage Open Communication:** Positivity promotes a more open and trusting environment, where team members feel comfortable sharing ideas and feedback.

Overcoming Negative Influences

- **Manage Stress Effectively:** Learn techniques to manage stress, as it can be a major source of negativity.
- **Avoid Negative Talk:** Steer clear of gossip and negative conversations, which can harm workplace morale.
- **Challenge Pessimistic Thoughts:** When faced with negative thoughts, challenge and reframe them in a more positive light.

Implementing Positivity in Your Career Path

- **In Job Interviews:** Display a positive attitude during interviews. Employers are often drawn to

candidates who exude optimism and enthusiasm.
- **On Your Resume:** Highlight achievements and experiences in a way that reflects a positive impact and attitude.
- **In Your Professional Network:** Be known in your network for your positive outlook. This reputation can open doors and create opportunities.

Balancing Positivity with Realism

While positivity is essential, it is crucial to balance it with realism. Being overly optimistic can sometimes lead to unrealistic expectations. Aim for a grounded optimism that acknowledges challenges but focuses on positive outcomes.

Positivity is more than just a pleasant attribute; it's a powerful tool that can transform work environments, enhance team dynamics, and contribute to personal and professional growth. In a world often filled with stress and challenges, a positive attitude can be a beacon of hope and resilience. By cultivating and demonstrating positivity, you not only improve your own work experience but also contribute significantly to the well-being and productivity of your team. Remember, positivity is a choice, and choosing it can open a world of possibilities in your career and beyond.

Trait #12: Problem-Solving
The Art of Overcoming Challenges

In the competitive world of employment, problem-solving stands out as a critical skill employers actively seek in candidates. This chapter explores the multifaceted nature of problem-solving and its profound impact on professional and personal arenas.

The Essence of Problem-Solving

Problem-solving is more than just finding solutions to issues; it's a comprehensive process that involves identifying problems, analyzing information, brainstorming alternatives, and implementing effective strategies. It's about being proactive, innovative, and resilient in facing challenges.

Why Employers Value Problem-Solving

- **Innovation and Improvement:** Effective problem-solving leads to innovative solutions and continuous improvement in processes and products.
- **Efficiency and Productivity:** Skilled problem-solvers can quickly identify and address issues, minimizing disruptions and enhancing productivity.
- **Leadership and Initiative:** Problem-solving is closely tied to leadership qualities. It demonstrates initiative and the ability to handle challenging situations.

- **Adaptability:** Solving problems effectively indicates adaptability, a key trait in today's ever-changing business landscape.
- **Collaborative Skills:** Problem-solving often involves teamwork, showcasing an individual's ability to work collaboratively.

Demonstrating Problem-Solving Skills

- **Share Specific Examples:** During interviews, discuss specific instances when you identified a problem and successfully implemented a solution.
- **Highlight Creative Solutions:** Emphasize situations where you developed creative or innovative solutions to complex problems.
- **Explain Your Process:** Talk about how you approach problem-solving. Outline the steps you take from identifying the issue to implementing a solution.
- **Show Results:** When possible, quantify the results of your problem-solving efforts to demonstrate their impact.
- **Demonstrate Logical Thinking:** Employers value a logical and systematic approach to problem-solving. Show how you use analysis and reasoning in your process.

Cultivating Problem-Solving Skills

- **Enhance Critical Thinking:** Develop your critical thinking skills. The ability to analyze and evaluate information is crucial for problem-solving.
- **Be Curious:** Cultivate a sense of curiosity. The work of asking questions and seeking to

understand 'why' and 'how' can lead to effective problem identification and solving.
- **Practice Creativity:** Engage in activities that stimulate creative thinking. Diverse perspectives often lead to more innovative solutions.
- **Learn from Others:** Observe how experienced colleagues and leaders solve problems. Learning from their approaches can provide valuable insights.
- **Embrace Challenges:** View challenges as opportunities to improve your problem-solving skills. The more you practice, the better you become.

Problem-Solving in Different Contexts

- **In Team Settings:** Show your ability to collaborate with others to find solutions. Team problem-solving can lead to more comprehensive and effective strategies.
- **Under Pressure:** Demonstrate your capacity to remain calm and think clearly under pressure, a valuable trait in crisis situations.
- **In Customer Service:** Highlight how you've used problem-solving to address customer issues, enhancing satisfaction and loyalty.

Balancing Problem-Solving with Flexibility

While being a good problem-solver is crucial, balancing it with flexibility and adaptability is equally essential. Solutions that work in one context may not be effective in another.

Overcoming Barriers to Effective Problem-Solving

- **Avoiding Jumping to Conclusions:** Take the time to fully understand the problem before attempting to solve it.
- **Dealing with Complexity:** Break down complex problems into smaller, more manageable parts.
- **Handling Stress:** Develop stress management techniques to help you maintain clarity and focus when solving problems.

Problem-Solving in Everyday Life

- **In Personal Relationships:** Use your problem-solving skills to navigate and resolve conflicts in personal relationships.
- **In Day-to-Day Decisions:** Apply these skills in your daily life, whether planning a trip or managing your finances.

Enhancing Your Resume with Problem-Solving

- **Highlight Relevant Experience**s: Include specific roles or projects where your problem-solving skills were crucial.
- **Use Action Words:** Use verbs like 'analyzed', 'resolved', 'implemented', or 'innovated' to describe your problem-solving actions.
- **Showcase Outcomes:** Emphasize the positive outcomes of your problem-solving efforts.

Problem-solving is an invaluable skill that transcends the boundaries of the workplace. It's about approaching challenges not as roadblocks but as opportunities for growth and innovation. In your career, showcasing your ability to solve problems effectively can set you apart as a proactive, resourceful, and valuable team member.

Beyond work, these skills can enhance your personal life, helping you navigate complex situations quickly and confidently. Remember, at the heart of problem-solving lies the ability to see the bigger picture, think critically, and act decisively. Cultivate this skill, and watch as it opens doors to new opportunities and successes in every facet of your life.

Trait #13: Self-Reliance

The Power of Initiative and Independence

In the diverse landscape of desirable traits for job candidates, self-reliance is crucial. This chapter delves into the nuances of self-reliance in the professional context and how it can significantly enhance your value as an employee.

Understanding Self-Reliance

Self-reliance in the workplace is about being proactive, self-motivated, and capable of working independently. It's not just about doing your job without supervision; it's about taking initiative, anticipating needs, and contributing effectively without needing constant guidance.

Why Employers Value Self-Reliance

- **Promotes Efficiency:** Self-reliant employees get things done efficiently, reducing the need for supervision and frequent check-ins.
- **Drives Innovation:** Self-reliant Individuals often take the initiative to develop new ideas and solutions, driving innovation within the company.
- **Enhances Team Dynamics:** Self-reliant team members can manage their responsibilities effectively, contributing to a more dynamic and productive team environment.
- **Indicates Leadership Potential:** Self-reliance is a crucial trait of influential leaders. It shows the

ability to manage oneself and potentially, in the future, manage others.
- **Reflects Professional Maturity:** Being self-reliant demonstrates professional maturity that makes you a dependable and valuable employee.

Demonstrating Self-Reliance

- **Show Initiative:** Take proactive steps in your role. Volunteer for new projects, suggest improvements and don't hesitate to express your ideas.
- **Ask Informed Questions:** During interviews, ask specific questions about your role and responsibilities. This shows that you are thinking ahead and are serious about contributing effectively.
- **Highlight Independent Achievements:** Share examples of projects or tasks you have completed independently, emphasizing your ability to work autonomously.
- **Demonstrate Problem-Solving Skills:** Show that you can identify problems and develop solutions on your own, an essential aspect of self-reliance.
- **Exhibit Confidence in Your Abilities:** Display confidence in your skills and judgment. This confidence is a crucial component of self-reliance.

Cultivating Self-Reliance

- **Develop a Wide Skill Set:** The more skills you have, the more capable you can handle diverse tasks independently.

- **Set Personal Goals:** Setting and achieving personal goals can build your confidence and ability to manage tasks independently.
- **Learn Continuously:** Stay updated with new developments in your field. Continuous learning is critical to remaining self-reliant in an ever-evolving professional landscape.
- **Seek Feedback:** Constructive feedback can help you understand your strengths and areas for improvement, guiding your journey toward self-reliance.
- **Embrace Challenges:** Facing and overcoming challenges is a fast track to becoming more self-reliant.

Self-Reliance in Different Work Settings

- **In Office Environments:** Take charge of your responsibilities and manage your workload effectively without needing frequent direction.
- **In Remote Work:** Demonstrate that you can stay motivated and productive even when you are not physically in the office.
- **In Leadership Roles:** Show that you can lead projects and teams with minimal oversight, setting a standard for others to follow.

Balancing Self-Reliance with Teamwork

While self-reliance is valuable, it is essential to balance it with teamwork. Be ready to collaborate and communicate effectively with others, recognizing that some tasks are best accomplished as a team.

Overcoming Barriers to Self-Reliance

- **Dealing with Uncertainty:** Develop strategies to handle uncertainty. This might include seeking mentorship or doing additional research to inform your decisions.
- **Managing Overdependence:** If you are too dependent on others, take small steps towards handling tasks independently.
- **Building Confidence:** Confidence is critical to self-reliance. Work on building your self-confidence through success in both small and large tasks.

Demonstrating Self-Reliance in Your Career Path

- **In Your Resume:** Include instances where you took the initiative or worked independently, highlighting the positive outcomes of your actions.
- **During Job Interviews:** Be prepared to discuss situations where your self-reliance was pivotal to the success of a project or task.
- **Through Professional Development:** Pursue additional training and certifications on your own initiative. This demonstrates a commitment to self-improvement and self-reliance.

Self-reliance is a multifaceted attribute that encompasses initiative, independence, and proactive problem-solving. It is a sign of a mature, dependable, and valuable employee in the workplace. Cultivating self-reliance makes you more attractive to potential employers and empowers you to take charge of your career and professional growth. Remember, being self-reliant doesn't mean you have to do everything alone;

it's about having the confidence and capability to handle responsibilities effectively, whether independently or as part of a team.

Trait #14: Teamwork

The Art of Collaborative Success

In the realm of sought-after qualities in job candidates, teamwork is a fundamental skill. This chapter unpacks the essence of teamwork, shedding light on why employers highly value it and how it can significantly impact your professional journey.

Understanding Teamwork

Teamwork is not just about working alongside others; it's about actively collaborating, communicating, and contributing to achieve a common goal. It involves the ability to compromise, support, and enhance the collective efforts of a group, creating an environment where the sum is greater than its parts.

Why Employers Value Teamwork

- **Enhances Problem-Solving:** Diverse teams bring together varied perspectives, leading to more comprehensive problem-solving.
- **Boosts Productivity:** Effective teamwork can streamline processes and improve productivity, as tasks are shared and goals are achieved more efficiently.
- **Encourages Innovation:** Collaborative environments are fertile grounds for innovation, as ideas are shared, developed, and refined through group input.
- **Fosters a Positive Work Environment:** Teamwork contributes to a positive and

supportive work culture, enhancing employee satisfaction and retention.
- **Reflects Adaptability:** Being an effective team player shows adaptability, an essential trait in today's dynamic work environments.

Demonstrating Teamwork

- **Share Team Success Stories:** During interviews, recount specific instances where you contributed to a team's success, highlighting your ability to collaborate and compromise.
- **Discuss Conflict Resolution:** Explain how you've handled conflicts within a team setting, showcasing your skills in negotiation and mediation.
- **Highlight Communication Skills:** Emphasize your ability to communicate effectively within a team, a key component of successful collaboration.
- **Show Empathy and Understanding:** Demonstrate your capacity to understand and respect different perspectives, an essential aspect of effective teamwork.
- **Exhibit Flexibility:** Display your willingness to adapt your role and responsibilities within a team as needed.

Cultivating Teamwork Skills

- **Engage in Team Activities:** Participate in group activities, both within and outside of work, to hone your teamwork skills.
- **Practice Active Listening:** Active listening is vital in understanding team members and contributing meaningfully to group discussions.

- **Develop Emotional Intelligence:** Emotional intelligence helps navigate team collaboration's interpersonal dynamics.
- **Seek Feedback:** Regularly seek feedback on your teamwork skills from team members and leaders.
- **Learn from Team Leaders:** Observe influential team leaders and learn how they foster collaboration and handle team challenges.

Teamwork in Various Settings

- **In Office Teams:** Contribute actively in meetings, offer assistance to colleagues, and share credit for successes.
- **In Remote Work:** Maintain clear communication, be responsive, and participate actively in virtual meetings and collaborations.
- **In Cross-Functional Teams:** Be open to working with colleagues from different departments, understanding and respecting their unique contributions.

Balancing Teamwork with Individual Responsibility

While teamwork is essential, balancing it with individual accountability is important. Ensure that your personal tasks and responsibilities are also handled effectively.

Overcoming Challenges in Teamwork

- **Navigating Group Dynamics:** Learn to navigate different personalities and work styles within a team.

- **Dealing with Conflict:** Develop conflict resolution skills to handle disagreements constructively.
- **Avoiding Groupthink:** Encourage open dialogue and the expression of diverse opinions to avoid conformity and foster innovative thinking.

Teamwork in Leadership Roles

- **Modeling Team Behavior:** As a leader, model the teamwork behavior you expect from your team.
- **Fostering Collaboration:** Create an environment where collaboration is encouraged and rewarded.
- **Building Team Cohesion:** Invest time in team-building activities to strengthen relationships and cohesion within the team.

Demonstrating Teamwork in Your Career Path

- **On Your Resume:** Highlight experiences demonstrating your ability to work effectively in teams, including any leadership roles within teams.
- **In Job Interviews:** Be prepared with anecdotes showcasing your teamwork skills, focusing on situations where your contribution significantly impacted.
- **In Professional Development:** Participate in workshops and courses focusing on team-building and collaborative skills.

Teamwork is a critical skill that transcends job descriptions and titles. It is about bringing your unique skills and perspectives to a group while valuing and leveraging the contributions of others. Being an effective team player in the modern workplace can significantly enhance your professional value, opening doors to new opportunities and experiences. Remember, the strength of a team lies in its members' ability to collaborate, communicate, and work towards common goals. Cultivate this skill, and watch as it transforms your career prospects and the quality of your professional interactions and achievements.

Trait #15: Work Ethic
The Foundation of Professional Excellence

A strong work ethic is often a non-negotiable for employers in the spectrum of qualities that shape an ideal job candidate. This chapter will delve into the nuances of work ethic and how it significantly impacts your professional standing and growth.

Understanding Work Ethic

A good work ethic is about more than just hard work; it encompasses values that include reliability, dedication, productivity, cooperation, and a sense of responsibility. It's about taking pride in your work and committing to delivering your best, consistently and conscientiously.

Why Employers Value Work Ethic

- **Reliability and Consistency:** Employees with a strong work ethic are reliable and consistent in their performance, making them invaluable assets to any team.
- **Positive Influence:** Such individuals often set a high standard in the workplace, inspiring others to follow suit.
- **Enhanced Productivity:** A robust work ethic directly translates to enhanced productivity and efficiency, contributing significantly to the company's goals.
- **Professional Growth:** Individuals with a strong work ethic are often open to learning and improvement, leading to continuous professional growth.

- **Trustworthiness:** A good work ethic builds trust. Employers trust diligent employees with essential tasks and responsibilities.

Demonstrating Work Ethic

- **Be Punctual and Reliable:** Always be on time, whether for a meeting, project deadline, or a regular workday.
- **Show Dedication:** Take on tasks with enthusiasm and dedication. Show that you are willing to go the extra mile when necessary.
- **Maintain High Quality of Work:** Ensure that the quality of your work is consistently high. Pay attention to details and take pride in what you deliver.
- **Communicate Effectively:** Keep your team and supervisors informed about your progress and any challenges you face.
- **Be a Team Player:** Cooperate and collaborate with your team. A good work ethic is not just about individual performance but also about contributing to the team's success.

Cultivating a Strong Work Ethic

- **Set Personal Standards:** Define what a good work ethic means to you and set personal standards accordingly.
- **Self-Motivation:** Develop self-motivation techniques to keep pushing yourself, especially during challenging times.
- **Time Management:** Effective time management is crucial to a good work ethic. Prioritize tasks and manage your time efficiently.

- **Seek Feedback:** Regular feedback can help you understand how your work ethic is perceived and where you can improve.
- **Balance Work and Rest:** While hard work is essential, balancing it with rest and rejuvenation is crucial to avoid burnout.

Work Ethic in Various Professional Settings

- **In Office Environments:** Take initiative, meet deadlines, and be a collaborative team member.
- **In Remote Work:** Show that you can be disciplined and productive without direct supervision.
- **In Leadership Roles:** Lead by example. A leader with a strong work ethic can inspire the entire team.

Showing Work Ethic During the Job Search

- **In Your Resume:** Highlight instances where your strong work ethic led to positive outcomes or recognition.
- **During Interviews:** Share specific stories that showcase your dedication, reliability, and commitment to quality.
- **Through References:** Choose references who can vouch for your work ethic and dedication to your previous roles.

Balancing Work Ethic with Personal Well-being

A strong work ethic should not come at the cost of your health and personal life. Strive for a balance that allows you to be productive but also leaves room for self-care and personal interests.

Overcoming Challenges to Maintaining a Good Work Ethic

- **Dealing with Burnout:** Recognize the signs of burnout and take steps to address it, such as talking to your supervisor, taking breaks, or seeking professional help.
- **Staying Motivated:** Find ways to keep yourself motivated, like setting short-term goals, celebrating small wins, or changing your routine.
- **Handling Monotony:** If your work becomes monotonous, find new challenges or learning opportunities within your role.

A strong work ethic is a cornerstone of a successful career. It's about committing to your responsibilities, striving for excellence, and being a reliable and productive member of your team. Cultivating a good work ethic not only increases your employability but also positions you for future opportunities and career advancement. Remember, your work ethic is a reflection of your professional identity. By nurturing this quality, you demonstrate not just your ability to perform a job well, but also your commitment to achieving excellence in all you do.

When These Qualities Become Problems
How An Unscrupulous Employer Can Use These Traits Against You

This book took entire chapters to detail fifteen great traits for an employer wanting to impress and maintain with suitable employers. But it will only have one chapter to highlight the dark side of coming into a workplace with all these tools where being a quality employee is a weird liability to bosses threatened people who can seem to get work done, even if competently. Look for these actions and habits in employers that will counter your ability to get things done, regardless of how well you master any of the fifteen traits.

Trait #1: Ambition

Ambition in an employee, typically a valued trait, can be exploited in several ways. Firstly, such employers might use an employee's ambition to manipulate them into accepting excessive workloads without commensurate compensation or recognition. Secondly, they could leverage this ambition to create internal competition, fostering a toxic work environment where employees are pitted against each other. Lastly, an unscrupulous employer may promise career advancement opportunities that they have no intention of providing, exploiting the employee's ambition to retain them under false pretenses.

Trait #2: Communication

There are scenarios where the trait of solid communication skills in an employee is to their disadvantage. Such employers may manipulate communicative employees into becoming the de facto mediators of workplace conflicts, burdening them with responsibilities beyond their role without additional recognition or compensation. They might also exploit these employees' abilities to communicate effectively by having them cover up or smooth over the company's internal issues, ethical lapses, or mistakes. Furthermore, an employer could use an employee's open communication style to extract personal or sensitive information, later using it against the employee in various workplace situations.

Trait #3: Confidence

Misusing an employee's confidence can result in turmoil in several detrimental ways. They might exploit this confidence by overloading the employee with responsibilities, assuming their self-assurance equates to an unlimited capacity for work. Such employers may also set unrealistic expectations or targets, capitalizing on employees' confidence to push them beyond reasonable limits. Additionally, a bad boss could manipulate a confident employee into taking risks or making decisions that benefit the employer at the expense of the employee's well-being or career prospects.

Trait #4: Critical Thinking

Turning the tables on employees' critical thinking skills can lead to real advantages for an employer, even to the detriment of the work that needs to be completed. By recognizing an employee's ability to solve complex problems, employers might overload them with the most challenging tasks without appropriate support or resources. This exploitation can lead to burnout and decreased job satisfaction. Additionally, the employer might manipulate the employee's critical thinking to justify making unethical decisions, framing them as logical necessities, thereby implicating the employee in morally questionable practices.

Trait #5: Dependability

Exploiting an employee's dependability is much simpler than you may realize. They may consistently assign extra work to dependable employees, knowing they are less likely to refuse, thereby overburdening them. Such employers might also take advantage of these employees' reliability by failing to provide adequate support or recognition, assuming they will continue to perform regardless. Additionally, a dependable employee could be kept in a stagnant role without opportunities for advancement, as their reliability makes them too valuable to lose in their current position.

Trait #6: Determination

ways to use employee's determination against them don't understand (or care) how harmful this is. They may recognize this trait and continuously set increasingly challenging goals, pushing employees to unreasonable limits. This can lead to the employee experiencing stress and burnout, as their determination is used to achieve the boss's ambitious targets without regard for their well-being. Moreover, such a boss could manipulate this determination, steering the employee towards tasks that serve the boss's agenda rather than the employee's career growth or the company's best interests.

Trait #7: Eagerness to Learn

It sounds as cruel as it is when an employer exploits an employee's eagerness to learn. They may assign excessive or overly challenging work under the guise of providing learning opportunities, overwhelming the employee without offering genuine support or mentorship. Such bosses might also manipulate this trait to have employees undertake tasks outside their job scope or skill level without proper training, thereby setting them up for failure. Additionally, they could promise future opportunities for growth and development that they have no intention of fulfilling, using this as a tactic to retain the employee under false pretenses.

Trait #8: Flexibility

Flexibility in employees should be a trait that is cherished, but some employers will quickly find reasons to exploit it. They may abuse this trait by frequently changing work schedules, job roles, or responsibilities at a moment's notice, causing undue stress and work-life imbalance. Such a boss could also impose unreasonable demands, knowing the employee's flexible nature will likely lead to surrender. Furthermore, they might take advantage of this flexibility by consistently assigning last-minute tasks, disregarding the employee's personal time or existing workload.

Trait #9: Honesty

A spiteful boss can manipulate an employee's honesty for their own benefit in several ways. They might exploit this trait by pressuring the employee to be complicit in unethical practices, leveraging their honesty to give credibility to questionable actions or decisions. Such bosses could also take advantage of an honest employee's transparency by using their admissions of mistakes or weaknesses against them, either in performance evaluations or to deny promotions. Furthermore, an employer could misuse an employee's honesty to gather personal or sensitive information, later using it as leverage in workplace negotiations or as a means of control.

Trait #10: Loyalty

There are plenty of ways to exploit an employee's loyalty that all lead to detrimental ends. They may use this loyalty to pressure the employee into accepting unreasonable workloads or hours, knowing they are unlikely to refuse due to their commitment to the job. Such bosses might also manipulate loyal employees into overlooking or even participating in unethical practices, leveraging their loyalty to override their better judgment. Furthermore, a vindictive boss could take advantage of a loyal employee's dedication by denying them opportunities for advancement, assuming they will remain with the company regardless of how they are treated.

Trait #11: Positivity

Trying to abuse an employee's positivity seems like an out idea, but this is a popular tactic of hostile bosses. They may exploit this trait by constantly delegating challenging or undesirable tasks to the employee, banking on their positive attitude to avoid confrontation or complaints. Such a boss could also dismiss or undermine legitimate concerns raised by the employee, labeling them as hostile and contrasting them with the employee's usually positive demeanor. Additionally, they might manipulate the employee's optimistic nature to mask a toxic work environment, using it to deflect from real issues that need addressing.

Trait #12: Problem-Solving

Strong problem-solving skills are usually a bonus to have in one's employees, but some employers see this trait as a threat to their authority. They may constantly assign the most challenging and stressful problems to the employee, exploiting their ability to handle difficult situations without providing adequate support or resources. Such a boss could also set unrealistic deadlines for problem resolution, putting undue pressure on the employee. They might need to acknowledge or reward the employee's problem-solving efforts, taking their skills for granted while piling on more responsibilities.

Trait #13: Self-Reliance

Exploiting your employee's self-reliance will always be a detriment to an entire organization. They may overload a self-reliant employee with work, taking advantage of their ability to manage tasks independently without offering necessary support or resources. Such a boss might also isolate the employee from team collaboration, leveraging their self-sufficiency to excuse a lack of team integration or assistance. Furthermore, an employee's self-reliance could be manipulated to deny them opportunities for training or professional development under the pretext that they can manage independently.

Trait #14: Teamwork

A strong commitment to teamwork keeps many organizations together through hard times, which is why turning the tables on this trait is as tragic as it is effective. They may burden a team-oriented employee with the bulk of group work, exploiting their cooperative nature and willingness to help others. Such a boss might also manipulate team dynamics to create an environment where the employee feels pressured to conform to unfair practices or decisions for the sake of team harmony. Additionally, they could use the employee's focus on teamwork to downplay their individual contributions, hindering their chances for recognition or advancement.

Trait #15: Work Ethic

The final trait highlighted as good for employees is also one of the most tragic bosses want to exploit: a strong work ethic. They may overload the employee with excessive work, capitalizing on their dedication and reluctance to refuse tasks. Such a boss could also set unrealistic deadlines and expectations, knowing the employee's commitment to their work will drive them to meet these demands at the cost of their well-being. Additionally, an employee's strong work ethic could be manipulated to cover up managerial inadequacies or understaffing issues, placing undue burden and stress on the employee.

About The Author
J Cleveland Payne

J Cleveland Payne is a highly accomplished author, renowned entrepreneur, distinguished military veteran, and seasoned media professional who has significantly impacted various fields. With a sincere dedication to personal and professional development, Payne has established himself as a multifaceted individual with a remarkable passion for empowering others.

With over 25 years of experience in traditional radio and television broadcasting, Payne has honed his skills in delivering captivating content and engaging audiences. However, his contributions extend far beyond the realm of media. As the founder and operator of Fast Forward Business Properties, LLC, Payne is committed to providing top-notch personal and professional development training, helping individuals and organizations unlock their full potential. Through his expertise, Payne equips his clients with essential skills and instills the confidence to navigate the ever-changing business landscape.

In addition to his notable work in training and development, Payne spearheads More Better Media, LLC. This dynamic media production company specializes in creating compelling audio, video, and written content. Whether it be through thought-provoking podcasts, visually engaging videos, or informative written materials, Payne excels at crafting content that resonates deeply with audiences, leaving a lasting impact.

Payne's background as an Air Force veteran plays a pivotal role in shaping his commitment to excellence and ability to connect with people. His military service instilled in him invaluable qualities such as discipline, attention to detail, and a strong work ethic, all of which continue to influence his entrepreneurial pursuits and interactions with others.

Payne has consistently demonstrated a steadfast dedication to continuous learning and growth throughout his illustrious career. By embracing new technologies, staying updated with industry trends, and always exploring innovative approaches, he delivers exceptional value to his clients and audience.

As a passionate advocate for personal and professional development, Payne strives to inspire individuals to reach their full potential, overcome challenges, and achieve their goals. His unique blend of experience in media production, training, and entrepreneurship allows him to provide practical insights and guidance to those seeking personal and professional growth.

To connect with J Cleveland Payne and benefit from his wealth of knowledge and expertise, you can visit his website at jclevelandpayne.net or email him at jclevelandpayne@gmail.com. His commitment to positively impacting and empowering others is evident in his online presence and his dedication to sharing his insights with those seeking his guidance.

About The Podcasts
Business Questions Answered Here & Two Minute Business Wisdom

J Cleveland Payne, a highly acclaimed author and seasoned entrepreneur, hosts the captivating podcast "Two Minute Business Wisdom," which provides small business owners with quick and actionable advice. In each episode, Payne shares invaluable insights, tips, and strategies that can be easily digested and implemented within their organizations, making it an indispensable resource for aspiring and established entrepreneurs.

As a companion to the top-rated podcast, "Business Questions Answered Here," "Two Minute Business Wisdom" offers concise and focused episodes that deliver crucial business wisdom in just two minutes. This format caters to the fast-paced nature of entrepreneurship, recognizing the time constraints small business owners face. By distilling his extensive experience across various industries and his personal and professional development expertise, Payne ensures that each episode delivers maximum impact within a short timeframe.

Listeners of "Two Minute Business Wisdom" can expect diverse topics covering essential aspects of running a successful business. From effective communication strategies and innovative marketing techniques to insightful leadership practices, productivity hacks, and efficient financial management, Payne covers it all. The podcast is a valuable toolbox of practical knowledge, empowering entrepreneurs to enhance their skills and make informed decisions in their day-to-day operations.

The podcast is intricately connected to its sister show, "Business Questions Answered Here," where small business owners worldwide submit their queries for Payne to address. This symbiotic relationship between the two podcasts ensures a comprehensive and well-rounded resource for business owners seeking practical advice and solutions to common challenges they encounter. Together, these podcasts create a dynamic platform for knowledge-sharing and community engagement.

To further amplify the impact of "Two Minute Business Wisdom" and "Business Questions Answered Here," Payne prominently features them on the website businessquestionsansweredhere.com. This website is a central hub of valuable resources, housing a vast collection of podcast episodes, articles, and additional content designed to empower small business owners and entrepreneurs [3]. It provides a one-stop destination for individuals seeking actionable insights and guidance to overcome obstacles and achieve their business goals.

Operating under the umbrella of More Better Media, LLC, Payne ensures that these podcasts deliver the highest quality content and serve as a beacon of inspiration for small business owners. More Better Media, LLC is deeply committed to producing engaging audio, video, and written content that informs, educates, inspires, and equips entrepreneurs with the knowledge and tools they need to thrive in their business ventures.

"Two Minute Business Wisdom" and "Business Questions Answered Here" collectively provide invaluable resources that empower small business owners to navigate challenges, make informed decisions, and succeed in their entrepreneurial endeavors. Whether you're seeking quick business wisdom or answers to your burning questions, these podcasts are essential companions on your journey to business excellence.

Made in the USA
Columbia, SC
08 January 2024